ALLEN COUNTY PUBLIC LIBRARY

1833 04502 3667

P9-ECK-957

WWI
FINAL YEARS OF
WORLD WAR I

JOHN HAMILTON

VISIT US AT
WWW.ABDOPUB.COM

Published by ABDO & Daughters, an imprint of ABDO Publishing Company, 4940 Viking Drive, Suite 622, Edina, Minnesota 55435. Copyright ©2004 by Abdo Consulting Group, Inc. International copyrights reserved in all countries. No part of this book may be reproduced in any form without written permission from the publisher.

Printed in the United States.

Edited by Tamara L. Britton
Graphic Design: John Hamilton
Cover Design: Mighty Media
Photos and illustrations:
    Corbis, p. 4, 5, 6, 7, 8, 10, 12, 13, 16, 19, 22, 23, 24
    John Hamilton, p. 7, 21
    National Archives, p. 1, 9, 11, 12, 14, 15, 16, 17, 18, 20, 24, 25, 26, 27, 28, 29
    Photos of the Great War, p. 28, 29
    Cover photo: Corbis

Library of Congress Cataloging-in-Publication Data

Hamilton, John, 1959-
    Final Years of World War I / John Hamilton
    p. cm.—(World War I)
    Includes index.
    Summary: An overview of the final years of World War I, emphasizing the role of the United States.
    ISBN 1-57765-915-5
    1. World War, 1914-1918—Campaigns—Western Front—Juvenile literature. 2. World War, 1914-1918—United States—Juvenile literature. 3. World War, 1914-1918—Participation, American—Juvenile literature. [1. World War, 1914-1918—United States.] I. Title

D522.7.H35 2003
940.4'31—dc21

2002033297

TABLE OF CONTENTS

A Separate Peace

Above: People in Petrograd, Russia, run away from government soldiers who were firing into the crowd, July 4, 1917. *Far right:* A poster from Russia's provisional government of 1917, with a slogan that says, "War Until Victory" *Below:* A portrait of Russian Tsar Nicholas II and his family

This is a war to end all wars.
   —American President Woodrow Wilson

Only the dead have seen the end of war.
   —George Santayana, Spanish American philosopher, in a counter to Wilson's words.

BY THE SPRING OF 1917, World War I had been dragging on for almost three years. In France, in the trenches of the Western Front, millions of soldiers had died or been horribly wounded in attacks that seldom gained any ground. The war was at a stalemate—yet the generals on both sides continued to send their men into battle, to an almost certain death.

By April, the morale of the French army finally cracked. Almost half of the French armed forces, 54 divisions, refused to fight. They threw down their rifles in protest, or simply disobeyed orders. The revolt of the French army was a serious crisis for the Allies. It took a change of command and several months of morale building to overcome.

Meanwhile, in Russia, another situation was spiraling out of control. Years of governmental corruption and oppression had fueled serious discontent among the Russian people. During World War I, crushing defeats by the German army made matters worse.

In February 1917, the Russian government finally fell apart. Russia's leader, Tsar Nicholas II, was forced to give up power. A loose collection of political parties then set up a provisional, or temporary, government led by Alexander Kerensky, who wanted to keep Russia in the war.

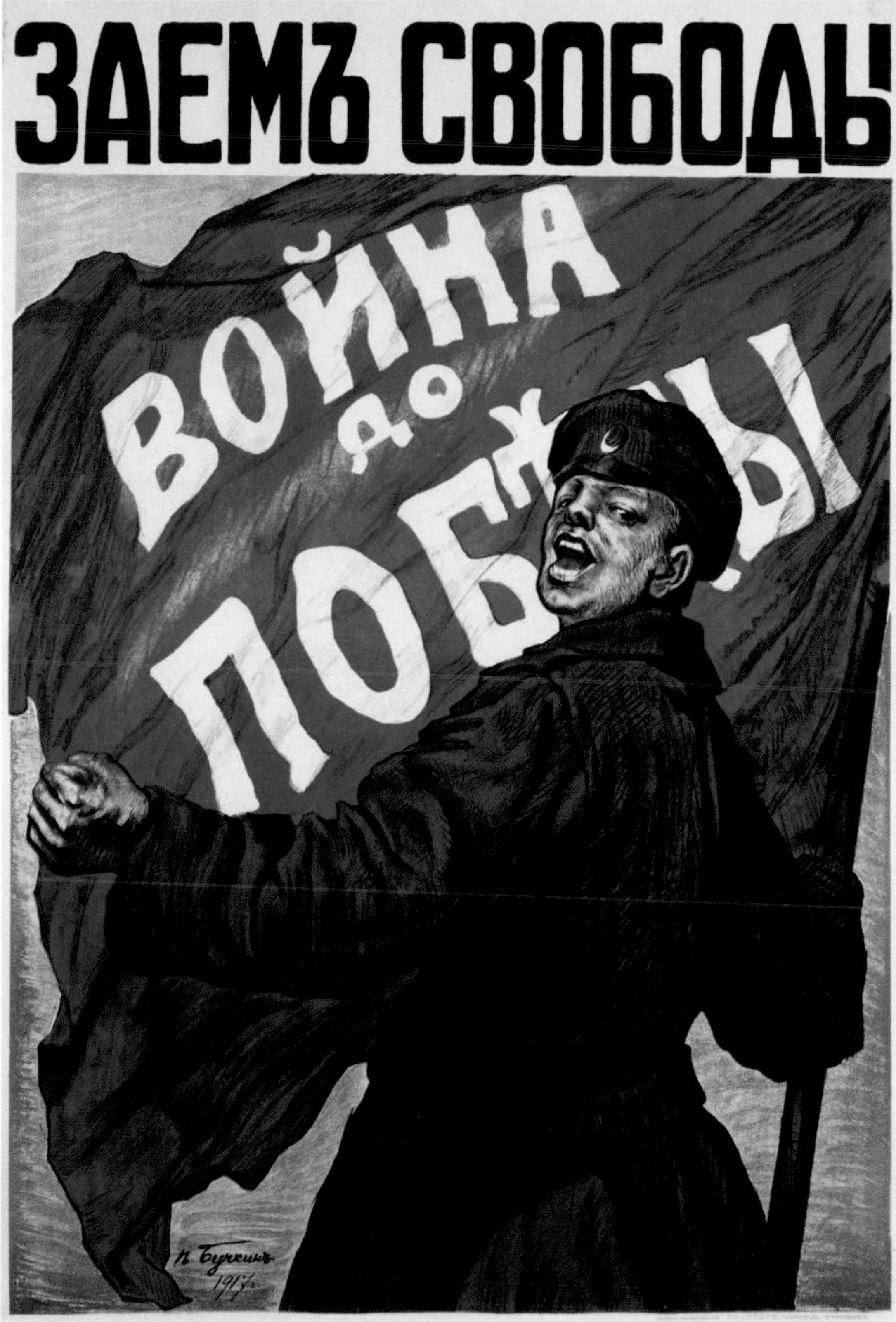

ЗАЕМЪ СВОБОДЫ
ВОЙНА
до
П. Бучкинъ
1917.

Right: Russian soldiers pose with patriotic banners, October 1917.

Although the government tried to keep fighting, things got worse for Russia. Supply lines of food and fuel broke down, creating shortages in the major cities. Citizens panicked and rioted in the streets. All over the country people became more and more desperate.

In October, Bolsheviks led by Vladimir Lenin seized control of the country and disbanded the provisional government. After the October Revolution—also called the Russian Revolution—the Bolsheviks set up a Communist government. People who disagreed with the government were often executed. The Communists did not want Nicholas II to try to reclaim power. So within a year, the Communists murdered the former tsar and his family.

The October Revolution caused the Russian army to disintegrate. It was replaced by the Red Army, and included soldiers who supported the Bolsheviks. Many soldiers deserted, or refused to follow orders. By the end of 1917, almost four million Russian soldiers had surrendered to the Germans or Austrians, further draining Russia of much-needed manpower. Lenin said that the soldiers "voted for peace with their feet."

The Bolsheviks wanted Russia to get out of the war. After seizing power, Lenin issued a Decree On Peace, which took Russia out of the war. Lenin did this without consulting with the other Allied powers. This is referred to as a separate peace. By the end of 1918, Russia had withdrawn from World War I and begun to collect its forces for the internal struggle to come. Russia would be engulfed in civil war for many months to follow as Lenin's forces, the Red Russians, fought soldiers

EUROPE ON THE EVE OF WWI, 1914

Atlantic Ocean

IRELAND

GREAT BRITAIN

London

English Channel

North Sea

NETHERLANDS

BELGIUM

LUX.

Paris

FRANCE

Bay of Biscay

PORTUGAL

SPAIN

Madrid

SPANISH MOROCCO

FRENCH MOROCCO

ALGERIA

TUNISIA

NORWAY

SWEDEN

DENMARK

Baltic Sea

GERMANY

Berlin

SWITZERLAND

ITALY

Rome

CORSICA

SARDINIA

SICILY

MALTA

Mediterranean Sea

FINLAND

Moscow

RUSSIA

Vienna

AUSTRIA-HUNGARY

Sarajevo

SERBIA

ALBANIA

GREECE

ROMANIA

BULGARIA

Black Sea

Adriatic Sea

CRETE

CYPRUS

OTTOMAN EMPIRE (TURKEY)

ARABIA

still loyal to the old provisional government, the White Russians. Eventually, America would even send thousands of combat troops, along with troops from several other countries, to fight on Russian soil against the Communists, but Lenin and his army would prevail.

Since it was no longer fighting Russia on the Eastern Front, Germany found itself with hundreds of thousands of battle-hardened troops that could be sent to the Western Front to fight the French and British. They could now launch one last huge attack that might win the war once and for all.

Things looked very bad for the Allies. But just when the situation looked the darkest, another event brought fresh hope. Across the Atlantic Ocean, the United States was preparing for war. If America could send enough troops in time, the tide of World War I might yet turn in favor of the Allies.

Below: Vladimir Lenin speaks in Moscow's Red Square in 1918.

AMERICA ENTERS WWI

WHEN WAR BROKE OUT in 1914, President Woodrow Wilson tried to keep the United States neutral, favoring neither side of the conflict. Even before the sound of the first gunfire rolled across the battlefield, there were already many Americans who didn't want their country to enter any kind of European war. These people, the isolationists, believed that anything that happened across the Atlantic Ocean was no concern to America. The U.S. seemed sheltered and safe, and the isolationists wanted to keep it that way.

There was another side to the argument, however. During the early part of the twentieth century, the United States saw a huge increase in immigration. Many of the immigrants were from European countries, and while loyal to their new home, they wanted to help their native countries. Political pressure to enter the war increased, but President Wilson was determined to keep the U.S. neutral.

By 1915, the United States was profiting by selling war materials and other goods to countries on both sides of the conflict. As a neutral country, it had a right to do this. But as the war dragged on, Germany's actions made it harder and harder for the United States not to choose sides.

Both Britain and Germany used their navies to disrupt enemy trade with other countries. Britain used its surface fleet to blockade German ports, while Germany attacked British merchant ships with submarines called U-boats. In 1915, Germany began unrestricted submarine warfare, sinking merchant ships and warships without warning.

Far right: U.S. officers pose at their headquarters in France in 1919. Captain Harry S. Truman, future president of the United States, stands in the second row, third from right.
Below: Anti-war activists march through the streets of New York City.

Right: The passenger liner *Lusitania* sinking after being attacked by a German U-boat on May 7, 1915.

On May 7, 1915, a German U-boat torpedoed and sank the British passenger liner *Lusitania*. The attack killed 1,198 people, including 128 Americans. The Germans claimed the ship was carrying weapons to England, but the sinking outraged many Americans. It was a public relations disaster for the Germans. President Wilson managed to keep the U.S. neutral, but sent strong diplomatic warnings to Germany. By the autumn of 1915, Germany stopped unrestricted submarine warfare for fear of drawing the U.S. into the war.

Germany had other image problems during the war. After its invasion of Belgium, some German soldiers were reported to have committed atrocities against civilians. In the eyes of neutral countries, especially in the U.S., these war crimes transformed the Germans into beastly "Huns."

Left: A German U-boat similar to the one that sank the *Lusitania*. Germany's use of unrestricted submarine warfare was a major mistake that eventually brought the United States into the war.

3 1833 04502 3667

10

The Germans also committed diplomatic blunders that pulled America closer to war. In January 1917, Germany announced that it would once again continue unrestricted submarine warfare against any ship, including those from neutral countries. The Germans were sure they could achieve victory over Britain within six months by choking off food and supplies. President Wilson protested this restriction of freedom of the seas by breaking off diplomatic relations with Germany. Wilson warned that if American ships were sunk, he would be forced to declare war.

Above: Actor Douglas Fairbanks encourages a crowd in New York City to purchase war bonds.

Above: A New York newspaper announces the U.S. entry into World War I. *Below:* President Wilson tells Congress on February 3, 1917, that the U.S. has broken official relations with Germany.

Then, in January 1917, the British intercepted a secret telegram sent by German Foreign Minister Alfred Zimmermann to Heinrich von Eckhardt, Germany's ambassador to Mexico. The telegram instructed von Eckhardt to offer Mexican president Venustiano Carranza an alliance if the United States entered the war. In exchange for its help, Germany promised to return to Mexico territories it had lost to the U.S., including Texas, New Mexico, and Arizona. The telegram was turned over to the United States, and on March 1, an outraged President Wilson made its contents public.

On March 16, German U-boats torpedoed two American ships. In the face of continued German aggression, Wilson felt he had no choice but to declare war. In a speech before Congress on April 2, 1917, Wilson said, "We will not choose the path of submission… The world must be made safe for democracy. Its peace must be founded upon the trusted foundations of personal liberty."

Congress voted overwhelmingly to support President Wilson. On April 6, 1917, the United States officially entered World War I.

Woodrow Wilson
(1856–1924)

Woodrow Wilson was the twenty-eighth president of the United States. First elected in 1912, he was reelected for a second term in 1916 under the slogan "He kept us out of war." Wilson struggled to keep America neutral, but by 1917 he was forced to use U.S. troops to stop German aggression.

A former president of Princeton University and governor of New Jersey, Wilson is often described as an idealist. His administration helped draft laws limiting unfair business practices, strengthening the nation's money supply, and outlawing child labor.

Wilson thought that World War I would be the war to end all wars. His Fourteen Points were proposals Wilson wanted passed after Germany surrendered in 1918. He wanted freedom of the seas, a reduction of weapons, and an end to the kind of secret diplomacy that started World War I. Wilson's last proposal was the formation of the League of Nations, an early form of today's United Nations. The League eventually was created, but it was weak and powerless. Wilson couldn't even persuade the United States to join.

Wilson went on a national tour to get the people's support for his Fourteen Points, but failed. Exhausted, he suffered a

Above: A portrait of U.S. President Woodrow Wilson *Below left:* President Wilson smiles from a train in St. Paul, Minn., on September 9, 1919, during a trip across the country to promote the League of Nations.

near-fatal stroke. Cared for by his wife, he served out the rest of his second term sick and bedridden. In 1919, he won the Nobel Peace Prize for his work in trying to bring peace to war-ravaged Europe. Woodrow Wilson died in 1924.

OVER THERE

Above: A riveter works at Hog Island Shipyard, PA, in 1918. When America entered the war, its industrial output rapidly accelerated. *Far right:* A U.S. soldier says good-bye to a loved one before shipping off to war in Europe.

WHEN GERMANY DECIDED in January 1917 to resume unrestricted submarine warfare, it took the risk that America would be drawn into the war. Most German military leaders, however, weren't worried about the United States. They thought they could win the war before large numbers of American troops reached the battlefields of France. Many didn't even think America would enter the war. And if it did, the military leaders argued that Germany was more than prepared to handle the threat.

German Admiral Eduard von Capelle, secretary of the navy, said in a speech to the German parliament on January 31, 1917, "They will not even come, because our submarines will sink them. Thus America from a military point of view means nothing, and again nothing and for a third time nothing."

The Germans underestimated the threat from America for several reasons. At the time, the American army ranked only seventeenth in the world in size. Doughboys, as U.S. troops were called, had no large-scale warfare experience since the Civil War, and had no heavy equipment other than machine guns.

With the declaration of war in April 1917, American industry kicked into high gear. The country had enormous potential in resources and manpower. By year's end, troops had been drafted, trained, equipped, and sent to France. Each month saw the departure of tens of thousands of fresh American soldiers. Unlike the soldiers of Europe, who were exhausted after years of war, the doughboys were enthusiastic and ready to fight. They believed they could win the war. By the war's end in 1918, over two million American troops were sent to fight, and not a single one was lost to German U-boat attacks, despite Admiral von Capelle's boasting.

The U.S. army in Europe was called the American Expeditionary Force (AEF). Its leader was General John Pershing. Pershing had proven himself to be a good leader during campaigns in Mexico and the Philippines. He had exceptional diplomatic skills, which would be an important factor in how the Americans fared in the war.

After Pershing and his staff arrived in France on June 14, 1917, Major Charles Stanton exclaimed, "Lafayette, we are here!" The Marquis de Lafayette was a French officer who helped America during the Revolutionary War. The statement captured the moment: the Americans had finally arrived to save the day, and the Allies—especially the French citizens—couldn't have been happier. They greeted the American troops with great enthusiasm.

Above: General Pershing arrives in France in 1917.

That enthusiasm didn't last long, however. The Allies were desperate to replace their dead and wounded soldiers with fresh American troops. But Pershing would have none of it. He wanted to build up a large American army and keep it under American command. The last thing he wanted was to send his doughboys into the meat grinder of the trenches to be killed senselessly. "We came American," said Pershing. "We shall remain American and go into battle with Old Glory over our heads. I will not parcel out American boys."

Right: Workers at a bomb factory

JOHN PERSHING
(1860–1948)

General John "Black Jack" Pershing began his military career as an officer in the Indian Wars, fighting the Apaches in the American southwest. He commanded the 10th Cavalry, a group of African Americans called Buffalo Soldiers. This was how Pershing got the nickname Black Jack.

Pershing also saw action in the Philippines, and was an observer in Japan during the Sino-Russo war. In 1916, he led the American expedition into Mexico to hunt down the revolutionary Poncho Villa.

Pershing had excellent battlefield skills and was courageous, and he was also very good at commanding large forces and getting things done. He could be cool and distant, but his men had great affection for him. Politicians didn't intimidate him, yet he remained flexible.

Above: General John Pershing

As commander in chief of American forces in World War I, he was determined to keep the AEF under his independent command. Even though the French and British resented this terribly, Pershing's wisdom was eventually proven as Americans began winning battles and pushing the Germans back.

Pershing wanted to train an army of at least one million soldiers before sending any into battle. But it would take time for that many American soldiers to arrive. Even though the Allies had treated Pershing like a savior when he first came, they soon grew bitterly disappointed when they realized how long it would take the Americans to be fully ready for battle.

Still, Pershing resisted Allied pressure and stuck to his plan. In the meantime, American troops trained hard, learning how to fight with hand grenades, heavy artillery, and poison gas. Their confidence rubbed off on the French troops, increasing their morale. By the summer of 1918, American troops were arriving at the rate of 250,000 every month.

FINAL PUSH

Above: A worker for the Salvation Army writes a letter home for a wounded U.S. soldier.

WITH MORE AND MORE fresh American troops arriving in France every day, the German High Command knew it had to act soon if it was going to win the war. Since 1917, Erich Ludendorff had been virtual military dictator of Germany. Earlier in the war, Ludendorff, working closely with Paul von Hindenburg, crushed the Russian army on the Eastern Front. After the failed offensive at Verdun in 1916, Ludendorff and Hindenburg were given command of the entire German army.

Beginning in March 1918, Ludendorff launched a dramatic series of attacks against the Allied lines. Breaking the tradition of static defenses in the trenches, the Ludendorff offensives were designed to strike quickly with devastating force. One goal was to drive a wedge between French and British forces. If the Germans quickly crushed the French, they hoped that the British would then also give up and sign a peace treaty. Most importantly, Ludendorff's plan called for the German army to accomplish all this before America could build a sizable force.

Right: U.S. soldiers hurl hand grenades at German forces. *Far right:* Louis Raemaekers' painting, *A Letter From the German Trenches*

Above: American soldiers fight at the Battle of Belleau Wood on June 3, 1918.

The Germans had developed new battlefield tactics that gave soldiers on the ground permission to make their own decisions. They also used elite storm troopers, who were specially trained and equipped for attacking.

When the first assault was launched on March 21, the Allies were caught off guard. The Germans rapidly broke through the trench lines and penetrated deep into French territory. During the first six weeks of fighting, the Allies lost more than 350,000 casualties. At one point the German army came within 40 miles (64 km) of the outskirts of Paris. The French panicked, and the government prepared to evacuate the capital for the second time during the war.

Although successful for the moment, the attacks came at a huge price for the Germans. Many men were killed, including most of the storm troopers. Their supply lines were stretched thin, and the men were exhausted. Instead of continuing on to final victory, the attacks fizzled out.

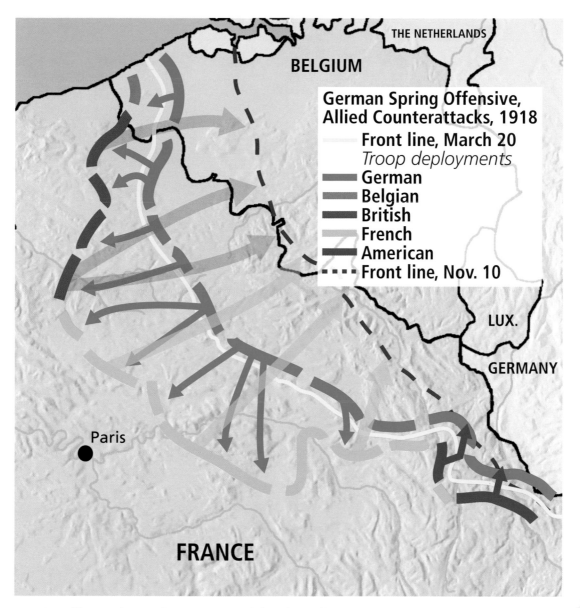

A map showing the German Spring Offensive and Allied Counterattacks, 1918, with labels for THE NETHERLANDS, BELGIUM, FRANCE, Paris, LUX., and GERMANY.

Legend:

German Spring Offensive, Allied Counterattacks, 1918
Front line, March 20
Troop deployments
German
Belgian
British
French
American
Front line, Nov. 10

A well-coordinated counterattack by the Allies soon reversed the German gains on the battlefield. General Pershing reluctantly released several thousand American troops to help thinly stretched French units battle the Germans. It was the first official engagement of the AEF in France. The Americans fought fiercely, especially U.S. Marines in the Battle of Belleau Wood. By August 1918, the shattered German army had been driven back, and forced to abandon all further offensive actions.

Above: A map shows the 1918 spring offensives by the German Army, and the Allied counterattacks.

NOTHING STOPS THESE MEN
LET NOTHING STOP *YOU*

UNITED STATES SHIPPING BOARD · EMERGENCY FLEET CORPORATION

Above: A U.S. recruiting poster urges men to join the army.

Far right: British soldiers pose at the newly captured St. Quentin Canal, a key stronghold of the German Hindenburg Line.

By now more than one million American troops were in France, ready for battle. After an impressive American victory at St. Mihiel, General Pershing joined forces with the French and attacked the Germans along the Meuse River and Argonne Forest of eastern France. The battle in the Argonne was the biggest fight of the war for the Americans. They cleared the forest of German defenders, but at a high cost. The doughboys lost 26,000 men killed, and another 100,000 wounded. The Germans suffered 100,000 casualties.

The Allies kept pounding at the German army. They pushed the enemy back to the Hindenburg Line, Germany's heavily defended line of trenches. At the end of September, British troops took control of the St. Quentin Canal, which was an important German stronghold. At last the Line had been broken. Soon the exhausted German army was forced to retreat. The Allies chased them across open country now, finally free from the trenches. The Germans' supplies were running low, and their spirits sank. The war was nearly at an end.

AFTERMATH

Above: German troops emerge from their trenches to surrender to Allied forces.

Far right: People celebrate the end of the war in Philadelphia, PA.

Below: The Belgian city of Ypres lies in ruins at the end of World War I.

We never really let the Germans know who won the war. They are being told that their army was stabbed in the back, betrayed, that their army had not been defeated. The Germans never believed they were beaten. It will have to be done all over again….
—General Pershing in 1923 on the prospects of another war

BY OCTOBER 1918, the German government realized that it would probably lose the war. Germany's allies, including Austria-Hungary and Turkey, quickly fell in the face of Allied attacks. As the German armed forces began falling apart, General Ludendorff advised the German emperor, Kaiser Wilhelm II, to negotiate for a cease-fire, or armistice.

On November 9, the kaiser gave up power and fled to Holland. Two days later, on the eleventh day of the eleventh month, at exactly 11:00 A.M., an armistice took effect between Germany and the Allies. The guns of war fell silent; four years of fighting had finally come to an end.

World War I had left nations exhausted and battle weary. A whole generation of young men had been killed or wounded on the field of battle. The armistice brought relief and joy around the world, but it was a bitter peace. Added to the cruelty of war was a horrible flu epidemic that struck in 1918–1919. The unsanitary conditions of war, plus the lack of medicines, helped spread the deadly disease. Worldwide, the flu killed more than 20 million people. In the United States, nearly 600,000 people died. In Germany, the terror of the flu epidemic was yet another misery that the people had to endure.

Early in 1919, allied leaders met at the palace of Versailles, near Paris, France, to decide on the conditions of surrender for Germany. In June of that year, the Treaty of Versailles was finally finished. President Wilson managed to get his Fourteen Points written into the treaty. He thought this would create a just and lasting peace. But French premier George Clemenceau was determined to punish and humiliate the Germans. He wanted them to pay for all that the French had suffered over the course of the war. British Prime Minister David Lloyd George also wanted to punish Germany. So Wilson's Fourteen Points were twisted into punishments for Germany, instead of steps toward lasting peace.

The treaty did provide for a League of Nations, Wilson's fourteenth point. The League was designed to prevent future wars by encouraging countries to solve their problems diplomatically. But member countries wouldn't cooperate with each other, and the League eventually failed.

The Treaty of Versailles was very harsh. Lloyd George and Wilson warned that if Germany were punished too much, it would only cause future trouble. Despite these misgivings, the treaty forced Germany to severely reduce its armed forces; give up large areas of land, including all its colonies; and pay astronomical sums of money in reparation for damage caused in the war. The Germans also had to accept all blame for the war.

Above: Allied leaders meet in Paris, France, in 1919 to write the Treaty of Versailles. From left to right: Prime Minister Lloyd George of Great Britain, Prime Minister Orlando of Italy, Premier Clemenceau of France, and President Wilson of the United States.
Right: The Aisne-Marne American Cemetery in Belleau, France

When the Versailles treaty was made public, the German people were shocked. They were told to accept the terms of the treaty or face more war. They had little choice but to accept.

Many Germans didn't believe the German army had actually been defeated. After all, Germany hadn't been invaded; the armistice took effect before the Allies entered German soil. Many Germans, including a young Adolf Hitler, believed that the German army had been "stabbed in the back" by corrupt politicians who had sold out their country.

The Treaty of Versailles caused great unrest in Germany. The country's economy was a shambles, and its weak government became very unpopular. The German people wanted new leaders who would restore national honor and dignity. Tragically, they eventually turned to Adolf Hitler and the Nazis. Instead of preventing future wars, the Treaty of Versailles set the stage for a second world war, which would prove to be even more terrible than the first.

Refugee children at Grand Val, near Paris, France, where a home was established for them by the American Red Cross in 1918

TIMELINE

1906 *February:* HMS *Dreadnought* is launched by Great Britain, beginning a worldwide naval arms race.

1914 *June 28:* Austria-Hungary's Archduke Franz Ferdinand is assassinated by a Serbian nationalist while touring Sarajevo, the capital of Bosnia-Herzegovina.

1914 *August:* World War I begins as German armed forces invade Belgium and France. Most of Europe, including Great Britain and Russia, soon enters the war.

1914 *August 26-31:* Russia suffers a major defeat at the Battle of Tannenberg.

1914 *September 9-14:* Second massive Russian defeat, this time at the Battle of the Masurian Lakes.

1915 Turkish forces slaughter ethnic Armenians living within the Ottoman Empire. The Turkish government accuses the Armenians of helping the Russians. Casualty totals vary widely, with estimates between 800,000 and 2 million Armenians killed.

1915 *Spring:* German Zeppelins launch bombing raids over English cities.

1915 *April 22:* Germans are first to use lethal poison gas on a large scale during the Second Battle of Ypres.

1915 *May 7:* A German U-boat sinks the unarmed British passenger liner *Lusitania*, killing 1,198 people, including 128 Americans. The American public is outraged, but President Wilson manages to keep the U.S. neutral.

1916 *February 21-December 18:* The Battle of Verdun. Nearly one million soldiers are killed or wounded.

1916 *July 1-November 18:* The Battle of the Somme costs approximately 1.25 million casualties. On the first day of the infantry attack, July 1, British forces suffered a staggering 60,000 casualties, including 20,000 dead, the largest single-day casualty total in British military history. Many troops are killed by a new battlefield weapon, the machine gun.

1917 *January 31:* Germany declares unrestricted submarine warfare, outraging the American public.

1917 *March 12:* The Russian Revolution overthrows Tsar Nicholas II.

1917 *April 6:* The United States declares war on Germany.

1917 *November:* Tanks are used for the first time on a large scale at the Battle of Cambrai. And on November 7, Russia is taken over by Lenin's communist government during the Bolshevik Revolution.

1917 *December 15:* Russia's Bolshevik government agrees to a separate peace with Germany, taking Russia out of the war.

1918 *March 21-July 19:* Germany mounts five "Ludendorff offensives" against strengthening Allied forces. The attacks are costly to both sides, but Germany fails to crush the Allied armies.

1918 *May 30-June 17:* American forces are successful against the Germans at Chateau-Thierry and Belleau Wood.

1918 *September 26-November 11:* French and American forces launch the successful Meuse-Argonne Offensive.

1918 *September 27-October 17:* British forces break through the Hindenburg Line in several places.

1918 *November 11:* Armistice Day. Fighting stops at 11:00 A.M.

1919 *May 7-June 28:* The Treaty of Versailles is written and signed.

GLOSSARY

ALLIES
Great Britain, France, and Russia formed the Allies in 1914 at the outbreak of World War I. Japan also joined the Allies, but played a minor role. Russia dropped out of the war in 1917. Italy joined the Allies in 1916, followed by the United States in 1917.

ARMISTICE
A formal truce, or cease-fire, during which a peace treaty is decided on and signed by countries fighting a war.

ARTILLERY
Large guns, too heavy to carry, that fire explosive shells at the enemy from a great distance. Coordinated artillery barrages can cause massive destruction without exposing friendly ground troops to enemy fire.

CASUALTIES
Soldiers killed or wounded in battle.

CENTRAL POWERS
During World War I, the Central Powers included Germany, Austria-Hungary, and Turkey. Bulgaria also joined the Central Powers later in the war.

DIPLOMACY
Peaceful relations between countries, including making treaties and trade agreements. In 1914, diplomacy failed, propelling most of Europe into declaring war.

EASTERN FRONT
Unlike the static trench warfare of the Western Front, the Eastern Front of WWI was characterized by large, sweeping maneuvers over open terrain. In the opening years of the war, Russian forces moved into Germany and Austria-Hungary, but by March, 1918, the German army penetrated deep into Russia.

Nazi

A member of the National Socialist Workers' Party. The Nazi political party, led by Adolf Hitler, a World War I veteran, controlled Germany from 1933 until the end of World War II, in 1945.

NEUTRAL COUNTRY

A country that doesn't participate in a war between other countries. Sometimes neutral countries bend the definition of the word. Even though the United States stayed neutral until 1917, it actively traded goods and weapons with both sides, although it had especially close economic ties with the Allied countries. In 1914, Belgium was a neutral country when the German army invaded on its way to France. This violation of neutrality drew Great Britain into the war.

STALEMATE

A chess term describing a situation in which it is impossible to move without exposing one's king to check, resulting in a draw. On the battlefield, a stalemate results when neither side can gain ground because each is so heavily defended. On the Western Front of World War I, a stalemate lasted for nearly four years, despite millions of soldiers losing their lives.

WESTERN FRONT

Established by December 1914, the Western Front was a network of trenches that stretched across eastern France and a section of western Belgium. The Western Front ran approximately 400 miles (645 km), reaching from the North Sea to the border of Switzerland.

WEB SITES

Would you like to learn more about the final years of World War I? Please visit **www.abdopub.com** to find up-to-date Web site links. These links are routinely monitored and updated to provide the most current information available.

INDEX